One World

THE HISTORY AND GOVERNMENT OF Sub-Saharan Africa

J.M. KLEIN

PowerKiDS press.

Published in 2021 by The Rosen Publishing Group, Inc.
29 East 21st Street, New York, NY 10010

First Edition

Editor: Caitie McAneney
Book Design: Seth Hughes

Photo Credits: Cover (top) Feroze Edassery/Shutterstock.com; cover (bottom) John Wollwerth/Shutterstock.com; p. 5 john images/Moment/Getty Images; p. 6 AFP/Getty Images; p. 7 Jeff Greenberg/Universal Images Group/Getty Images; p. 9 https://commons.wikimedia.org/wiki/File:0910_6290l_Blacksmith_bellows,_Fang,_Gabon_(5618228668).jpg; p. 10 Bridgeman Art Library/Image Partner/Hulton Fine Art Collection/Getty Images; pp. 12, 36 (top) Print Collector/Hulton Archives/Getty Images; p. 14 W. and D. Downey/Hulton Royals Collection/Getty Images; p. 15 Stock Montage/Archive Photos/Getty Images; p. 16 DEA/G. DAGLI ORTI/De Agostini/Getty Images; p. 17 Culture Culb/Hulton Archive/Getty Images; p[. 18 (left) https://upload.wikimedia.org/wikipedia/commons/e/e8/1813_Thomson_Map_of_Africa_-_Geographicus_-_Africa-thomson-1813.jpg; p. 18 (right) https://upload.wikimedia.org/wikipedia/commons/4/43/Africa1898.png; p. 19 Photo 12/Universal Images Group/Getty Images; p. 23 GIANLUIGI GUERCIA/AFP/Getty Images; p. 24 (top) Scott Peterson/Hulton Archive/Getty Images; p. 24 (bottom) YASUYOSHI CHIBA/AFP/Getty Images; p. 25 GYSEMBERGH Benoit/Paris Match Archive/Getty Images; pp. 26, 27 Scott Peterson/3rd Party-Agents/Getty Images; p. 29 Keystone/Hulton Archive/Getty Images; p. 30 (top) David Turnley/Corbis Premium Historical/Getty Images; pp. 30 (bottom), 35 Popperfoto/Getty Images; p. 31 Louise Gubb/Crobis Historical/Getty Images; p. 32 City Press/Gallo Images/Getty Images; p. 33 PHILIP LITTLETON/AFP/Getty Images; p. 36 (bottom) ASHRAF SHAZLY/AFP/Getty Images; p. 27 Wendy Stone/Corbis Historical/Getty Images; p. 38 AFP/Getty Images; p. 39 LUIS TATO/AFP/Getty Images; p. 41 Mark Cuthbert/UK Press/Getty Images; p. 42 https://upload.wikimedia.org/wikipedia/commons/7/77/Constitution_of_Botswana_1966.jpg; p. 43 ALBERT GONZALEZ FARRAN/AFP/Getty Images; p. 44 AFP/Getty Images; p. 45 (top) Robertus Pudyanto/Getty Images Entertainment/Getty Images; p. 45 (bottom) Heritage Images/Hulton Archive/Getty Images.

Cataloging-in-Publication Data
Names: Klein, J.M.
Title: The history and government of Sub-Saharan Africa / J.M. Klein.
Description: New York : PowerKids Press, 2021. | Series: One world | Includes glossary and index.
Identifiers: ISBN 9781725321366 (pbk.) | ISBN 9781725321380 (library bound) | ISBN 9781725321373 (6 pack) | ISBN 9781725321397 (ebook)
Subjects: LCSH: Africa, Sub-Saharan–Juvenile literature. | Africa, Sub-Saharan–History–Juvenile literature. | Africa, Sub-Saharan–Politics and government.
Classification: LCC DT351.K545 2021 | DDC 967–dc23

Manufactured in the United States of America

CPSIA Compliance Information: Batch #CSPK20: For Further Information contact Rosen Publishing, New York, New York at 1-800-237-9932

CONTENTS

Introduction

SUB-SAHARAN AFRICA

Composed of hundreds of different groups of people and formed by thousands of years of history, sub-Saharan Africa is rich with diverse cultures and nations. About 48 different countries are part of the region, which is south of the Sahara, the largest hot desert in the world.

Today, governments in those countries range from democracies like South Africa, to countries torn apart by civil war like the Democratic Republic of Congo and Sudan. While the nations of sub-Saharan Africa have each had their own histories and governments, they have all been shaped by the impact of European colonialism.

diverse: Different or varied.

colonialism: Control by one power over a dependent area or people.

The fight for the many rich resources found in sub-Saharan Africa led to the division of Africa by European leaders—a division which still impacts the region today. Even after countries throughout the area established their independence, the effects of colonialism were far reaching. The shadow of colonialism influences religion, culture, and language, and still leads to violence, civil war, and **human rights** violations, or wrongdoings.

Some governments in the area are still unstable. However, democracies are emerging throughout sub-Saharan Africa and economies are growing as the region moves beyond colonial structures.

With some of the oldest civilizations in the world, sub-Saharan Africa is a large and diverse area south of the Sahara Desert. People disagree about how many countries are included in the region, but the World Bank recognizes 48 countries.

human rights: Universal rights possessed by all people in the world because they are a human being.

Chapter One

THE CRADLE OF HUMANITY

Sub-Saharan Africa is often called the "cradle" of humanity because it is where human history began. Scientists believe the first humans came from either eastern or southern Africa.

History in FOCUS

In Ethiopia in 1974, scientists found fossils believed to be more than three million years old. Named Lucy, the skeleton belonged to an *Australopithecus*, a primate species believed to be an ancestor of humans.

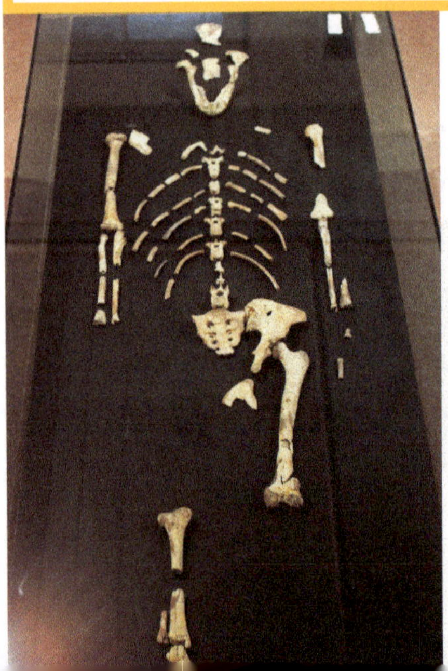

A skeleton scientists named Lucy is the oldest fossil evidence of human ancestors.

Between 200,000 to 400,000 years ago, *homo sapiens*—or modern humans—appeared in sub-Saharan Africa. Early humans migrated from Africa between 60,000 to 100,000 years ago. Eventually they reached every continent in the world except Antarctica.

Scientists found fossils of early human ancestor species in caves in South Africa. Some are as old as 2.8 million years.

As early humans migrated, they discovered language, learned to make fire, and built semi-permanent settlements. **Nomads** planted crops, such as yams, as they wandered across Africa.

migrate: To move from one region to another.

About 2,000 years ago, many Bantu-speaking people from west Africa migrated to east Africa. Bantu people are part of the same native African language group, which includes Swahili. The migration of the Bantu people changed the linguistic, or language, traditions of sub-Saharan Africa. Most of the people of east Africa had been hunter-gatherers or herders, but the Bantu people brought ironwork–including tools and weapons–and agriculture with them.

THE SUB-SAHARAN ORAL TRADITION

Sub-Saharan history is primarily preserved through Africa's oral traditions, rather than through books or written material.

In west Africa, poets and musicians called griots served as human record keepers. Griots told stories by performing them. They performed stories about births, marriages, deaths, hunts, battles, and the histories of kings. Each village had its own griot, but a griot would also often know the history of other nearby villages.

Today, hip-hop music and dance mimics, or copies, the rhythmic spoken-word storytelling performed by griots. Griots, such as Mory Kanté from Guinea, are still famous as artists in west Africa and have had international careers.

Ancient civilizations and settlements flourished in sub-Saharan Africa. As early as 500 BC, both iron and agriculture became important to the Nok people, who lived in today's Nigeria. Each Nok town had a king who ruled over groups made of large families.

In the 2nd and 3rd centuries, the kingdom of Axum (or Aksum) controlled trade routes between the Mediterranean Sea and Asia. Axum lasted until around the 8th century AD, and was the first sub-Saharan kingdom to make its own coins.

The Bantu civilization of the Swahili people in east Africa was made up of **city-states**. The city-states made up a network of trade ports. Each city-state was ruled by its own king.

People from the Bantu-speaking language group brought ironwork like this blacksmith bellows as they migrated from west Africa.

city-state: A political division made up of a city and surrounding area.

In west Africa, kings ruled. Ghana was the first great west African empire, founded around the 4th century AD. It was replaced by the kingdom of Mali, a powerful and rich kingdom. Mali's largest city was the famed city of Timbuktu, a wealthy trading city and center of learning and culture. In the Mali empire, the mansa, or king, ruled with the assistance of elders and local chiefs.

Mali ruler Mansa Musa is still considered the richest person of all time. Reports on his wealth helped plant the idea amongst Europeans that Africa was a land of gold—which would eventually lead to Europeans stealing that wealth five centuries later.

Mansa Musa is considered to be the richest person in history. Mansa Musa ruled the wealthy empire of Mali. The Mali empire lasted from around 1240 to 1645.

THE ENSLAVEMENT OF SUB-SAHARAN AFRICANS

Over the course of five hundred years, almost 20 million sub-Saharan Africans were enslaved by Europeans and Arabs.

In the 14th century, Portuguese explorers arrived in west Africa while searching for new trade routes to Asia. By 1444, the Portuguese forcibly removed sub-Saharan Africans as slaves. This ultimately led to the development of the transatlantic slave trade. Between the 16th and 19th centuries, as many as 12 million Africans were forcibly removed and taken to the Americas as slaves. About 15 percent died on the journey through the Middle Passage. Sub-Saharan Africans were also enslaved in the Middle East, India, Egypt, the Arabian Peninsula, and North Africa.

Millions of sub-Saharan Africans were forcibly taken from their homelands, and many were brought to the "New World" in the Americas.

NUMBER OF SLAVES IMPORTED FROM AFRICA

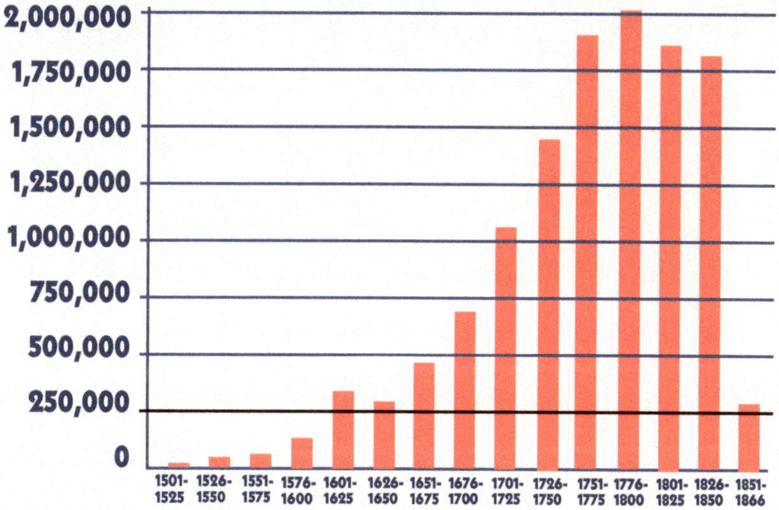

Middle Passage: The sea route traveled by slave ships from west Africa to the West Indies.

History in FOCUS

Enslaved west Africans brought folktales and proverbs to North America, making them a part of the culture. These stories included the African tradition of a "trickster tale," a story where an animal or human outsmarts another character.

Many sub-Saharan Africans died on packed, dirty ships on their way to the Americas. The survivors, who were enslaved, brought their culture with them.

Chapter Two

THE DIVISION OF AFRICA

Ivory. Rubber. Copper. Cotton and timber. In the 19th century, sub-Saharan Africa overflowed with abundant and rich natural resources—and European nations wanted them. This led to European imperialism, a period when nations in Europe sought to increase their power by gaining control over other countries.

natural resource: Something in nature that people can use, such as plants, minerals, water, and soil.

imperialism: A policy by which a country increases its power by gaining control over other areas of the world.

KING LEOPOLD'S BRUTAL RULE OF THE CONGO

Under colonial rule, Africans experienced hardship and brutal treatment. The Congo, possessing some of the richest natural resources in Africa, suffered greatly.

King Leopold II of Belgium claimed and gained control over the Congo in 1885 and forced the Africans living there to collect rubber and ivory. Belgians punished local workers with **mutilation** if they didn't collect enough rubber each day. Under Leopold's rule, an estimated 10 million people died—half the population of the Congo—and many more were disabled.

King Leopold ruled the Congo for more than 20 years until the Belgian government forced him to give up control in 1908 because of international outrage.

King Leopold II of Belgium controlled a massive area in the sub-Saharan region. He named it the Congo Free State, and his forced rule led to nearly 10 million deaths.

mutilation: An act of removing or severely damaging a limb or other body part of a person or animal.

A 1906 political cartoon illustrates the poor treatment of people native to the Congo under the rule of King Leopold II.

With the **Industrial Revolution** booming in Europe, European nations wanted to control and secure sources of raw materials needed to fuel their growing economies. Sub-Saharan

Africa was a strong source of cotton, iron, and other needed natural resources, as well as gold and diamonds. So many countries sought control of the continent that it was known as the "scramble for Africa."

The invention of a new rubber tire helped spur the demand for automobiles during the Industrial Revolution. Rubber was one of the most valuable resources in sub-Saharan Africa during colonization. This picture shows rubber harvesting.

To avoid fighting amongst themselves, leaders of 14 European countries met to create rules about how to divide up the continent at a conference in Berlin, Germany, in 1884 and 1885. They wanted to make sure they could control Africa's resources—at the expense of the Africans who owned those resources.

At the time, only the outskirts of Africa were colonized. About 80 percent of Africa was still independent—under traditional and local rule—including most of the interior. At the Berlin Conference, leaders of European nations spent three months carving up Africa—without the input of African leaders. They divided Africa into 50 countries, with France, Belgium, Germany, and Great Britain getting the bulk of the land.

History in FOCUS

Ethiopia was the only part of the sub-Saharan region not colonized during the scramble for Africa. Ethiopian emperor Menilek II defeated invading Italian colonizers in 1896 after first trading for modern weapons and ammunition.

Menilek II of Ethiopia defeated an invading Italian army, making Ethiopia one of the only countries in sub-Saharan Africa not colonized.

However, the new map of Africa created by the European leaders didn't take into account any of the more than 1,000 **indigenous** cultures and governments of Africa. The European leaders formed countries and territories by drawing lines on the map—which divided some groups of people and merged other groups that didn't get along.

A map of Africa in 1813 (left) shows that most of the continent was not divided into countries. But in an 1898 map, Africa is divided into countries following European colonization.

indigenous: Describing groups that are native to a particular region.

The conference formalized the scramble for Africa, which led to a 20-year period of intense colonization. Countries including France, Belgium, Germany, and Great Britain fought to gain control of various parts of the sub-Saharan region, stealing land from the resisting Africans.

European leaders at the Berlin Conference in 1884 divided Africa, deciding which country got each parcel. The leaders drew lines on maps without considering African cultures or tribes.

Almost all of Africa was colonized by Europeans. There were only four independent countries in Africa until 1950. In sub-Saharan Africa, only Ethiopia and Liberia—formed by freed American black slaves in 1821—were free.

SUB-SAHARAN AFRICAN INDEPENDENCE

After World War II, a big push for independence in sub-Saharan Africa began. The war led to a rise in African nationalism. The European political climate also changed. In the wake of World War II, it was harder for Europe to argue that countries in Africa should remain colonies, given the defeat of imperialist Nazi Germany.

Called the "father of African nationalism," Ghana president Kwame Nkrumah campaigned for the **liberation** of Africa, resulting in Ghana's independence from Great Britain in 1957. Nation after nation followed over the next two decades.

History in FOCUS

In 1960, so many African countries gained independence that it was called "the year of Africa." That year, 17 sub-Saharan African countries became independent, including Mali, Senegal, the Democratic Republic of Congo, Madagascar, and Nigeria.

nationalism: Loyalty and devotion to one's nation.

Chapter Three

ETHNIC CONFLICT AND HUMAN RIGHTS

The **decolonization** of sub-Saharan Africa proved to be a challenge. Under colonial rule, many Africans didn't receive education or leadership opportunities and didn't have necessary experience to form new governments. Many groups who had been forced together now ran into conflict. One of the most severe examples was in the countries of Rwanda and Burundi, formerly one Belgian colony. Colonization there caused ethnic conflict, which would lead to genocide.

ethnic conflict: Tension between two groups with different ethnicities.

genocide: The systematic killing of a particular ethnic group.

HUMAN RIGHTS IN SUB-SAHARAN AFRICA

Civil wars in sub-Saharan Africa are one reason human rights violations remain a widespread problem throughout the region. The United Nations (UN) says that human rights are rights that belong to all humans—no matter their race, sex, nationality, ethnicity, language, or religion. All humans are entitled to basic rights, including life and liberty, freedom from slavery and torture, freedom of opinion and expression, and the right to work and learn—no matter what.

In addition to Rwanda and the Democratic Republic of Congo, countries where human rights violations have been especially bad include Togo and Sierra Leone.

History in FOCUS

Beginning in 1991, an 11-year-long civil war in Sierra Leone led to numerous human rights violations and killed 70,000 people. Soldiers on both sides attacked civilians, not just soldiers. Both sides also forced children to be soldiers.

Rwanda was home to two primary ethnic groups–the Hutus and the Tutsis. German, and later Belgian, colonizers believed the farmer Hutus were the working class and the cattle herder Tutsis were royalty, therefore more fit to rule. Even though the Tutsis were a much

ethnicity: A group that shares common cultural traits, such as language.

smaller group, the colonizers put the Tutsis in charge of the Hutus. Tutsis received better education and controlled most of the resources.

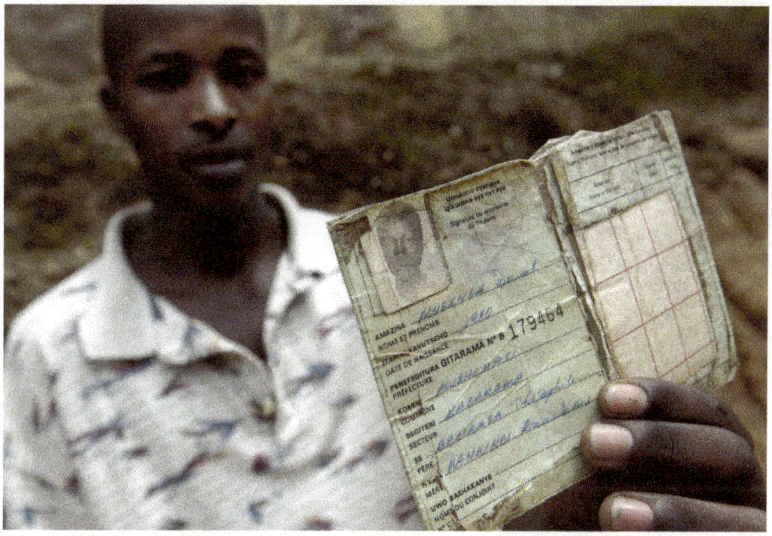

The Belgian government made Rwandans carry ethnic identity cards after World War I, which showed whether they were Hutu or Tutsi. The Belgians put the Tutsis in charge of the Hutus, which led to ethnic conflict.

The Hutus, who were the majority of the population, resented the Tutsis being in charge. They rebelled against Belgium and the Tutsis in power in 1959. During the Rwandan Revolution, Hutus forced about 150,000 Tutsis out of the country, to Burundi. By 1962, Rwanda and Burundi became independent countries, with Belgium withdrawing its control. Hutus continued to kill and expel Tutsis.

Hutu militia members and civilians attacked Tutsis during the genocide, trying to get rid of the entire ethnic group.

Ethnic tensions continued to worsen—the Tutsi army killed 80,000 to 200,000 Hutus in Burundi in 1972. In 1994, the Rwandan Genocide claimed the lives of 800,000 to 1 million people, in only 100 days.

Memorials like this show the impact of the 1994 genocide. Between 800,000 and 1 million people were killed in just 100 days.

Many people were killed in their own villages by neighbors or people they had known their whole lives.

When the Tutsi rebel army successfully expelled the Hutu militia, conflict spread. Nearly two million Hutu **refugees** evacuated, or left, their country. They fled to the Democratic Republic of Congo, then called Zaire.

After Rwanda's genocide, refugees evacuated into nearby Zaire, today's Democratic Republic of Congo. This would lead to a major war in Zaire, as surrounding countries also got involved.

refugee: A migrant person who flees their homeland to escape disaster, persecution, or war.

More than 2 million refugees fled Rwanda after the 1994 genocide. The Tutsi government regained control and the Hutus feared the Tutsis would retaliate, or get even, for the genocide.

Among the refugees were militia members responsible for the killings. Those militia members then attacked Tutsis living in the Congo. The Rwanda Tutsi government invaded Zaire, killing Hutus in refugee camps.

History in FOCUS

Experts believe the Rwandan genocide could have been prevented or stopped if United Nations countries had stepped in. In 2005, these countries signed the Responsibility to Protect, agreeing they had a responsibility to protect the world from future genocides.

This led to a conflict sometimes called "Africa's first world war," as nearby Zimbabwe, Namibia, and Angola joined the fighting in Zaire. More than five million people died between 1994 and 2003, mostly of starvation or disease.

Refugees filled camps like this in Zaire, now the Democratic Republic of Congo. A civil war between 1994 and 2003 was the bloodiest conflict after World War II. More than five million people died, mostly of starvation or disease.

THE GOVERNMENT'S RESPONSIBILITY TO PROTECT HUMAN RIGHTS

Governments of all nations must promote and protect human rights and the fundamental freedoms of everyone. That's the core belief of the United Nation's International Human Rights Law.

The Hutu-led Rwandan government failed to meet that obligation when it encouraged its citizens to attack the Tutsis. By directly engaging in and ignoring the numerous human rights violations, the Rwandan government was guilty of abusing human rights.

After the genocide, the UN Security Council established an international court—the first to pass judgment on genocide. The International Criminal Tribunal for Rwanda listened to over 3,000 witnesses. They **indicted** 93 people, including military, government officials, and religious leaders

Chapter Four

APARTHEID AND SOUTH AFRICA

For more than 50 years, apartheid dominated the country of South Africa. Apartheid, Afrikaans for "separateness," is a system of racial segregation.

THE ROOTS OF APARTHEID

Apartheid became official law in 1948, but its roots go back to South Africa's history of colonialism and slavery.

Dutch settlers used slavery to colonize South Africa and once slavery was outlawed, used discrimination to keep black South Africans working in gold and diamond mines for low wages.

In 1902, Dutch-descended **Afrikaners** lost to the British in the Boer War, and South Africa became a British colony. Anti-British feelings led to nationalism. Afrikaners believed South Africa was their "God-given homeland" and that the white race was superior. They saw black South Africans as a threat because there were significantly more non-white South Africans than white South Africans.

apartheid: A system of legal racial segregation that existed in South Africa under which the rights of the majority "non-white" inhabitants of the country were restricted.

segregation: The forced separation of races or classes.

From 1948 to 1994, the South African government established different rules for white people and non-white people. Public facilities such as parks or restrooms were separated for whites and for non-white people. Marriage between white people and non-white people was not allowed. Under apartheid, black South Africans had to carry identification papers known as passbooks—which limited where they could go—at all times. They also had strict curfews.

Signs in public places identified where non-white South Africans were not allowed. Public places were separated for whites and non-white people.

Apartheid served as a way for white people to control black people—and to make sure white-owned mining companies had cheap black labor. The apartheid system divided black South Africans into ten different "homelands" where they had to live. The homelands were

Under apartheid, black South Africans had to carry passbooks, which restricted where they could go. The passbooks identified the districted "homeland" where its holder lived. Black South Africans were not citizens anywhere other than their homeland and could not vote.

overcrowded and didn't have jobs, which forced black South Africans to take low-paying migrant jobs or to work in mines. It was also illegal to strike, or protest against employers.

Black South Africans protest apartheid in 1952. Violent police acts against peaceful protesters led to international outrage, which helped end apartheid.

When they were not in their specific homeland, black South Africans were not citizens. They had no **political rights** and could not vote. Schools were also separate. Black schools got a fraction of the funding of white schools and were designed to push black students into low-paying jobs.

political rights: Rights to participate in government, which include the right to hold public office and the right to vote.

History in FOCUS

Anti-apartheid leaders like Nelson Mandela were essential to ending apartheid. Arrested for treason in 1961 for his protests against apartheid, Mandela continued to work from prison for 27 years, until his release in 1993.

Nelson Mandela was president of South Africa from 1994 to 1999. Mandela spent 27 years in prison after being arrested for protesting apartheid and was the first black and the first democratically elected president in South Africa.

Black South Africans, especially students, resisted and protested apartheid. They boycotted white businesses and staged nonviolent protests. But these protests were met with violence. In 1960, South African police killed 69 peaceful protesters in Sharpesville, leading to more protests. In 1976, around 10,000 black students

treason: The crime of trying to overthrow a government.

marched to protest a new apartheid law. Police officers killed more than 100 of the protesters. The protests caught the attention of people around the world, and the international attention pressured the government to end apartheid.

High school students in Soweto, South Africa, march to protest a new apartheid law in 1976. As many as 10,000 students protested. South African police used force to break up the protest, wounding around 1,000 protesters and killing more than 100.

THE TRUTH AND RECONCILIATION COMMISSION

After apartheid ended in 1994, South Africa needed to heal from all the violence caused by division. To help, South African leaders formed the Truth and **Reconciliation** Commission. Archbishop Desmond Tutu, a human rights activist, led the commission, which sought to hold people responsible for human rights violations committed under apartheid.

For more than seven years, some 2,000 people told the commission what had happened to them during apartheid. Most of those people were victims. More than 7,000 people also asked for **amnesty** for what they had done during apartheid. The commission granted amnesty to around 1,000 people who showed remorse, or regret, to family members of people they had killed.

Archbishop Desmond Tutu leads the Truth and Reconciliation Commission in 1996. From 1995 to 2002, the commission heard stories about what happened during apartheid to expose the truth and bring reconciliation to South Africa.

In 1994, South Africa held its first fully democratic election, where both white and black South Africans could vote. The political party responsible for apartheid lost. Anti-apartheid leader Nelson Mandela became the first black and the first democratically elected president of South Africa. Apartheid officially ended and South Africa created a new **constitution** that wasn't ruled by racial discrimination.

History in FOCUS

Today, South Africa is a democratic country with a constitution protecting human rights. However, inequality still exists. White South Africans generally have more money and resources, including farmland, than black South Africans.

discrimination: Unfair treatment of people because of their race or beliefs.

Chapter Five

RELIGION IN SUB-SAHARAN AFRICA

Conflict between Christians and Muslims in parts of sub-Saharan Africa sparked decades of civil war and religious **persecution**. The conflict continues today in Sudan.

THE SPREAD OF CHRISTIANITY AND ISLAM

Christianity and Islam are dominant, or major, religions throughout the sub-Saharan region. They are practiced by thousands of people in addition to traditional African religions.

Axum King Ezana converted to Christianity in the 4th century, establishing Christianity in Ethiopia. Christianity's popularity declined as strong trade routes between North Africa and west Africa helped spread Islam. North African Berbers were early converts to Islam and traded with west Africans, exchanging salt for gold. Sudanese merchants adopted Islam in the 7th century and Islam became the religion of the upper class. Islam spread south to Ghana and Mali in the 13th century as the kings of west Africa became followers of Islam.

Missionaries to Africa, such as British **missionary** *and explorer David Livingstone, spread Christianity through the sub-Saharan region in the 19th and 20th centuries.*

Once the biggest country in Africa, Sudan is geographically divided between Muslims and Christians. Those living in the north of Sudan are primarily Muslim and Arabic-speaking. Those in the English-speaking South are a mix of Christian faiths and native religions. When the British colonized Sudan in 1898, they governed the North and the South differently. The North received money, investment, and education, while the South did not. The North and the South worked together to become independent. However, when they gained independence in 1956, the political, economic, and cultural differences between them proved too great.

missionary: Someone who travels to a new place to spread their faith.

History in FOCUS

Mansa Musa of Mali was the first west African ruler to make a religious pilgrimage to Mecca in 1324. Musa helped spread Islam, bringing scholars and architects to Mali to build mosques.

Mali king Mansa Musa made a religious pilgrimage to Mecca in 1324. He traveled more than 4,000 miles (6,437.4 km), bringing thousands of people, including soldiers, slaves, and attendants, and an incredible amount of gold.

South Sudan hoped for more **sovereignty** after independence but were instead governed by the North. Fighting between the regions began almost immediately and led to a series of civil wars lasting decades. Around 1.5 million people died, and millions of refugees fled Sudan.

Sudanese president Omar al-Bashir governed Sudan under a harsh interpretation of Islamic law until he was removed in April 2019. The International Criminal Court has accused him of numerous human rights violations.

In 1989, North Sudan established an **authoritarian government**—a kind of **unlimited government**—under the control of President Omar al-Bashir. President al-Bashir ruled Sudan under a harsh interpretation of Sharia, or religious laws, based on Islam's holy book, the Koran. Under al-Bashir, Christians faced discrimination and persecution. Women also had limited rights, and could be forced into marriage as young as the age of ten. People faced severe punishment for breaking Sharia.

Children known as the "Lost Boys of Sudan" arrive at a refugee camp in 1991. Civil war between Sudan and South Sudan created millions of refugees, including thousands of children who lost their parents.

South Sudan gained its independence from the North in 2011 and became a separate country. That was supposed to end the fighting.

authoritarian government: A government with a strong central rule where people have limited political and personal freedom.

unlimited government: In an unlimited government, control is placed solely with the ruler and their appointees, and there are no limits imposed on their authority.

But the treaty separating the countries did not address border areas. Fighting continues in the area between North and South Sudan, called the Nuba Mountains. The bulk of Sudan's oil resources are also in the South, leading to increased fighting over oil.

People in Sudan, including many women, protested the rule of Sudan President Omar al-Bashir throughout 2018 and 2019. Sudan's protests led to the removal of al-Bashir in April 2019 and the repealing of the Islamic law governing Sudan in November 2019.

Other conflicts in Sudan have created 2 million refugees, and killed more than 200,000 people. After al-Bashir's rule led to **inflation**, Sudanese people, including many women, protested. In April 2019, al-Bashir was removed as president by the military in a **coup d'état**. More protesting followed. In November 2019, Sudan's military authorities repealed, or did away with, Sharia. They ordered that al-Bashir's government be dissolved.

History in FOCUS

The arrival of the Portuguese in Nigeria in the 15th century reintroduced Christianity—which had never left Ethiopia—to the sub-Saharan region. During the 19th and 20th centuries, missionaries spread Christianity throughout the region.

RELIGIOUS CONFLICT OVER RESOURCES

In Nigeria, religious differences have deepened conflicts over scarce resources. Land is becoming scarcer as the population of Nigeria—already the largest in Africa—grows. As desertification and soil erosion further limit fertile land, farmers are moving onto land previously used by cattle herders.

In addition to being from different ethnic groups, the farmers are typically Christians and the herders are typically Muslim. In 2015, an estimated 2,000 Nigerians died because of fights between farmers and herders. Nigeria also faces conflict and religious persecution from Boko Haram, an Islamic extremist terrorist group.

A farmer and his son work on a Nigerian farm. Land in Nigeria is growing scarcer and causing fights between Christian farmers and Muslim cattle herders.

desertification: The process of fertile land turning into desert, usually caused by overgrazing.

erosion: The physical process in which soil and rock is moved by wind or water.

Chapter Six

EMERGING GOVERNMENTS AND AFRICA TODAY

Following their independence, many sub-Saharan countries experienced coup d'états, where power was taken over by the military, or **juntas**. The Central African Republic has been unstable since its independence and the Republic of Congo has experienced civil wars and military conflicts. Angola, a major oil-producing nation, saw a 27-year civil war following its independence.

History in FOCUS

African kings are still important as ceremonial figures. Kings like King Otumfuo Osei Tutu II, the traditional ruler of the Ashanti people of Ghana, serve as political and spiritual **heads of state**. Swaziland King Mswati III is the last absolute monarch—a ruler with unlimited power—in Africa.

Swaziland King Mswati III is one of the last few absolute monarchs in the world. He has ruled Swaziland since 1986 with power over the political system and the military.

While many countries struggled after independence, new systems of government and free economies are still emerging in sub-Saharan Africa. Countries are slowly developing **limited governments** led by their citizens.

A REGION OF MANY LANGUAGES

The sub-Saharan region is one of the most language-diverse regions in the world. More than 2,000 languages are spoken by different ethnic groups!

In Nigeria, people speak 520 different languages. Zimbabwe has 16 official languages, the most in the world. Many people speak a Bantu—or African indigenous—language, such as Swahili, in addition to English or French. English and French are both official and unofficial languages in the majority of the region because of the influence of Great Britain, France, and French-speaking Belgium during colonialism.

limited government: In a limited government led by the citizens, everyone, including all authority figures, must obey the laws.

Botswana and Senegal are considered the "success stories" of decolonization because they were two of the few countries that formed stable governments early on. Botswana has the longest- running democracy in Africa. Since its 1966 independence, Botswana has had a stable democratic government free of human rights abuses. Senegal has had three major political transitions since independence in 1960, but they have all been peaceful.

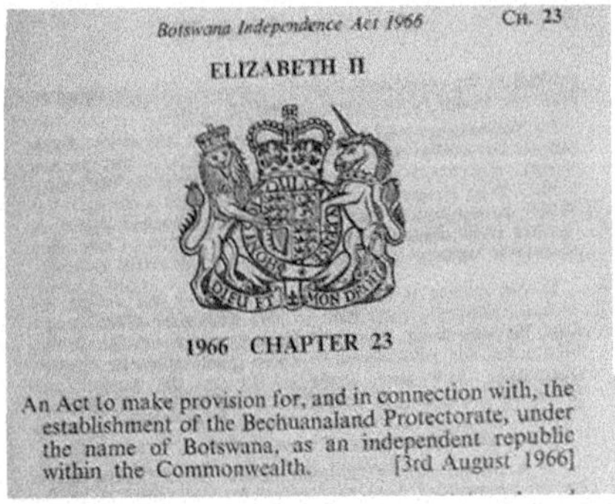

Botswana Independence Act 1966 CH. 23

ELIZABETH II

1966 CHAPTER 23

An Act to make provision for, and in connection with, the establishment of the Bechuanaland Protectorate, under the name of Botswana, as an independent republic within the Commonwealth. [3rd August 1966]

The 1966 Constitution of Botswana allowed the country to have a stable democratic government after its independence from Great Britain.

Other democracies are developing in the sub-Saharan region, but those newly democratic countries are not yet quite stable. After independence, Nigeria went back and forth between military **dictators** and civilian-led governments. Nigeria became a democracy in 2011, but still faces violence and political issues such as unfair elections.

United Nations peacekeeping missions are active in countries with unstable governments and violence. Active United Nations peacekeeping missions are in the Democratic Republic of Congo, Sudan, South Sudan, Mali, and the Central African Republic.

More limited governments are leading to economic growth. In Rwanda, the government used to control coffee production. The government removed taxes and legal restrictions and created a **free market economy**, meaning Rwandan farmers can now trade with buyers.

Much of the economy in sub-Saharan Africa remains based on selling natural resources or crops. Many people survive on subsistence farming. A lack of infrastructure like roads, transportation, and electricity hinders economic growth. European colonists built

subsistence farming: When farmers grow crops to feed themselves or their families for survival and not to trade.

infrastructure: The equipment and structures needed for a country, state, or region to function properly.

roads to and from mines in order to transport diamonds and gold out of the region, but they neglected transportation between villages. Countries like the Democratic Republic of the Congo and Chad have the potential to be rich countries because of their amount of natural resources—but remain poor because they can't develop those resources.

Only 7 percent of the roads in the Democratic Republic of Congo are paved. A lack of infrastructure like roads makes it hard for the country to access and develop the extraordinarily high amount of natural resources found there.

A region rich in resources, languages, traditions, and cultures, sub-Saharan Africa is finding its way. With its colonial past behind, sub-Saharan Africa now has the chance to develop its governments and march toward a better future.

History in FOCUS

The COVID-19 global pandemic, which started in 2019, put stress on governments in this region and around the world that will continue to have lasting effects.

SUB-SAHARAN INFLUENCES ON CULTURE

African culture spread as European colonizers returned to Europe and as enslaved Africans brought their culture to the Americas. African sculptures of the human figure influenced European artists like Henri Matisse and Pablo Picasso in the early 1900s and helped define early modern art. African sculptures showed the human figure as abstract rather than realistic. That inspired other artists to also use more abstract and spiritual elements in their art.

African music and dance influenced rap, hip-hop, and jazz. It's also the root of dances like the Charleston, the Lindy Hop, and the Twist. Sub-Saharan Africans continue to influence the world with their customs, art, music, dance, and folklore.

African music and oral storytelling influenced dance and music, and can be found throughout modern music, including in hip-hop, rap, gospel, and rock and roll.

Statues made by African artists showed the human figure in abstract rather than realistic form. This influenced European artists in the early 1900s and led to the development of modern art.

abstract: A thought or idea that isn't connected to a physical object.

GLOSSARY

Afrikaner: A person born, raised, or living in South Africa whose first language is Afrikaans and whose ancestors were Dutch.

amnesty: An act by which a pardon is granted to a group of people.

constitution: The basic laws by which a country or state is governed.

coup d'état: A sudden attempt by a small group of people to take over the government, usually through violence.

decolonization: The process of making a colony independent.

dictator: Someone who rules a country by force.

free market economy: An economy based on supply and demand with little or no government control.

head of state: A public person who represents a country, sometimes ceremonially.

indict: To formally decide that someone should be put on trial for a crime.

Industrial Revolution: An era of social and economic change marked by advances in technology and science.

inflation: A continual increase in the price of goods and services.

junta: A military group controlling a government after taking control of it by force.

liberation: The act of setting something or someone free.

nomad: A person who wanders from place to place to find shelter and food.

persecution: Making a group of people suffer cruel or unfair treatment.

reconciliation: The act of restoring harmony or settling differences.

sovereignty: The right to self-government.

FOR MORE INFORMATION

BOOKS:

Kamkwamba, William, and Mealer, Bryan. *The Boy Who Harnessed the Wind*, Young Reader's Edition. New York, NY: Puffin Books, 2017.

Krensky, Stephen. *DK Life Stories: Nelson Mandela*. New York, NY: DK Publishing, 2019.

Noah, Trevor. *It's Trevor Noah: Born a Crime: Stories from a South African Childhood* (Adapted for Young Readers). New York, NY: Delacorte Books for Young Readers, 2019.

WEBSITES:

Animated Atlas of African History
www.brown.edu/Research/AAAH/map.htm
Brown University provides an animated atlas of African history, showing the way the African map changes and evolves by year, as country borders change over time.

Great Grooves
thisworldmusic.com/gahu-african-drumming-and-dance-from-ghana/
Interactive audio mixers and a series of educational posts on drumming in west Africa allow visitors to this website to experience and learn about African music and dance.

PBS Learning Media, Africa's Great Civilization
ny.pbslearningmedia.org/collection/africas-great-civilizations/
Video clips, support materials, background, discussion questions, and activity ideas about the history of Africa are available through PBS.

INDEX